Eddy The Teddy Stands Up To Bullying

**Written & Illustrated
By**

H.B. Scribbles

Copyright © 2019 by Bookaholic Publishing
All rights reserved. No part of this book may be reproduced, scanned,
or distributed in any printed or electronic form without permission.
First Edition: Feb 2019
Printed in the United States of America

Hi, my name is Eddy the Teddy and I am on a mission that may get a little unsteady, however, I am ready, ready to stand up to Bad Boy Billy. This may sound mean or a little silly, but right now my good friend Billy is being a BIG BAD BULLY…

BAD BOY BILLY!

Bad Boy Billy runs up on the scene acting a little mean yelling, "Chirp-Chirp you snore like an old rusted machine!"

Eddy the Teddy puffs his chest out and stands up high to defend his friend and gives out a stern reply, "Bad Boy Billy please be wise and stop the bullying before you make someone cry!"

Big Bad Boy Billy flees faster than the wind and faster than the breeze. Bad Boy Billy stops in his tracks to eat and to think, *My sunglasses help me not to blink and my slick words get me attention…Should I stop… NAH!!! And that is one thing I do not need to doublethink*, he thought without a single blink.

Bad Boy Billy spots his other friend, Monk the Monkey, and teases again, "FOUR EYES!!!" Monk the Monkey feels confused and surprised.

Eddy the Teddy leaps up to defend his friend again, "Bad Boy Billy please stop the flip flop of your words that you choose to drop. Bullying is bad and you must stop!"

In a super flash, Bad Boy Billy takes off running. Chirp-Chirp and Monk the Monkey were stunned and buzzing. Bad Boy Billy didn't care. He thought it was a big old nothing, *hmm, maybe I should go bump something*, he thought as he continues running.

After a short sprint Bad Boy Billy spots Rookie the Turtle eating a fresh-baked cookie, "Looky-Looky, there is Rookie eating a delicious chocolate chip cookie and all it takes is a little bump-bump-bumpy to make me lucky!!"

After a fast bump and a quick lump Rookie lost his cookie to Bad Boy Billy. Rookie feels really sad and dizzy.

Eddy the Teddy races to stand by his friend Rookie and raises his arms high into the sky, "BAD BOY BILLY STOP, OH, STOP BEING A BIG BAD BULLY!!!" He shouted in a graceful outcry.

Bad Boy Billy dashes away and finds a quiet place to sit, *Am I a bully? Should I quit?... No! Eddy the Teddy should cool it, I mean, he is the only one saying I should stop and quit... Like, my other friends have yet to throw such a fit,* he thinks with a slice of whit.

Bad Boy Billy takes a moment to rewind and check on his friend Chirp-Chirp and what he heard blew his mind and sound like a bad crime.

"That Ba-Ba-Bad Boy Billy is a good friend of mine…But, but, why did he make fun of me during my bedtime. It wasn't fair and boy oh boy it feels like I've been through a nightmare." Chirp-Chirp said to himself with no due care.

Bad Boy Billy feels quite sad after seeing his friend Chirp-Chirp huffed-up and mad so he decides to stroll on to find Monk the Monkey his best lad.

Monk the Monkey is grumpy and a tad mad, "How can Billy be so bad… We are best friends… best comrades…"

Bad Boy Billy couldn't believe his ears. He snuck away to find Rookie, the same Rookie he recently stole the chocolate chip cookie from and as he approaches him his thoughts became quiet and wooly.

Rookie the Turtle couldn't speak or mumble, walk or tumble because of his friend Bad Boy Billy's actions were truly hurtful. Rookie couldn't help himself but sigh and cry.

Bad Boy Billy wonders off to lower his head to cry, *I didn't mean to be a bad guy… I miss my friends from the ground to the sky… Please, forgive me for this bad boy disguise… I miss my friends… I miss Eddy the Teddy, Chirp-Chirp, Monk the Monkey and Rookie… I am truly sorry about that delicious cookie…*

I AM SORRY!!!
PLEASE FORGIVE ME GUYS!!!

All of Billy's friends heard his cry, heard his pleas, all through the forest and all through the threes. Chirp-Chirp, Monk the Monkey, Rookie and Eddy the Teddy gather around Bad Boy Billy to see if he was ready, ready again to be great friends.

They knew Billy wasn't really bad, they seen it was just a misunderstood phase, and they knew he was just seeking attention, but in the wrong ways. Billy learns a valuable lesson and that lesson is Bullying never pays.

His friends gather close and look him directly in his eyes,

"Billy, we love you!!!"
They all said in sync as their smiles all rise to the beautiful sky.

Important Message About Bullying:

(Parents Please Read to Your Children)

Some kids just want attention..

Some kids just want love..

Some kids just do not know how to express themselves correctly..

Some kids do not get a lot love at home..

Some kids just want a good friend or two..

Never count someone out, especially if they are acting like a bully. Show them a little attention. Show them a little love. Teach them how to express themselves the right way. Be their friend and show them the true meaning of friendship.

Brighten Up Lost Love Yesterday Ignite Noble Gestures
TODAY!!!

www.ingramcontent.com/pod-product-compliance
Lightning Source LLC
Chambersburg PA
CBHW042137030726
47599CB00002B/505